Restless Soul Syndrome

The Search for Purpose and Meaning

Karolee Krause, LPC, SAC

TABLE OF CONTENTS

Purpose and Meaning.................... 11

Loss of Self 21

Relationships 29

Anger 43

Health and Wellness.................... 55

Grief and Loss 61

Visions 65

Trauma 69

Spirituality 73

Addiction 79

Validation 85

Life Transitions 89

Stress 97

Kindness 107

Everything has Purpose 111

Dedication

For Timothy

"It's your road, and yours alone. Others may walk it with you, but no one can walk it for you."

     Rumi

Preface

Enter the world of psychotherapy and the search for purpose and meaning. Through individualized therapy sessions, explore common everyday struggles with career, life changes, relationship conflicts, grief and loss.

As a Licensed Professional Counselor, I work extensively in the fields of Psychology and Mental Health and have noted a similar theme in counseling. We all search for purpose and meaning. Some people simply question, while others search a lifetime.

I have listened to thousands of stories of betrayal, business failures, relationship breakdowns, and spiritual depletion.

I have witnessed fear of moving forward, inability to release and let go of suffering, and resistance to change.

Restless Soul Syndrome is an exploration into our internal search for purpose and meaning in everyday life through a series of individual therapy sessions with people from all backgrounds, ages and ethnicities. The names of clients have been changed to protect their identify.

Purpose and Meaning

Brian, a 35-year-old male client reports wanting to die. He struggles finding purpose and meaning in his life and says there is no point in living. He never stops searching. He begins to give up hope.

"I want to grow a root out of here." Brain said.

"Can you explain what you mean by that?" I asked.

"I see my life as a tree. I've been firmly rooted here for so long that life no longer has meaning."

The client goes on to express that he seeks greener pastures elsewhere, convinced that happiness lies somewhere else. I explain that happiness and fulfillment do not lie in specific locations but are found within.

Because Brian feels grounded like a tree, he is unable to move forward or grow; therefore, he seeks meaning in other places.

In psychotherapy, an interior shift must take place before an exterior shift may occur. Until then, a move to a new geographical location will only bring temporary, short lived euphoria, eventually ending when unhappiness and discontentment return.

Feeling that our lives have greater meaning is part of the human experience. We all want to know that what we are doing is making a difference. People struggle to a greater or lesser extent. We often associate meaning with a career or profession and believe that our jobs are what make our lives meaningful. Yet I have worked with numerous people who have worked their entire lives in high profile jobs, only to realize they were in the wrong profession. Purpose is found in all aspects of life, not solely career.

Sometimes the search for meaning happens early and sometimes it happens later in life. I have personally searched for decades.

Our careers do not determine our happiness or our purpose in life. Life is a paradox because what we seek isn't always what we find.

◆

John, a middle-aged medical doctor with over 20 years' experience, was struggling with major depressive disorder. In the initial stages of counseling, he reported that he was having an affair with a woman for the past ten years.

Therapy sessions primarily focused on reasons for going outside of his marriage, but eventually turned to his underlying depression, which directly influenced John's poor decision making.

"I hate my job," John stated.

"As a physician?" I questioned.

"Yes, it was never what I wanted to do with my life. My father wanted me to be a doctor, so I went to medical school," he said looking down at the floor.

John reported that he was miserable in his career as a medical doctor. He had a successful practice and worked long hours, yet this was not his dream; it had been his father's goal. John became a doctor to make his father happy. He struggled for years finding purpose and meaning in a career that was not his calling, nor did he have passion for. He had never developed a sense of what he wanted to do in life, but simply followed someone else's visions that led him into a life of unfulfillment and severe depression.

Through a series of questions, John was asked what it was that he wanted to do or what held meaning for him. He said he wanted to quit his practice and retire. Because he had gone into the profession for the wrong reasons, life no longer held purpose or joy for him. His own personal search for meaning came to an end, and eventually a serious depression set in as he could see no way out. John began to have thoughts of suicide.

As we shifted from relationship issues and focused on creating a purposeful life, John informed me that his partner in the medical practice was resigning, which meant that he would have to take on all of his partner's patients.

Already overworked, stressed out and miserable in his profession, the doctor's depression worsened. He felt that he had missed his calling in life and had traveled down the wrong career path. He expressed regret that it was now too late to change direction due to having established himself as a prominent physician within the community and could not change professions at this point in his life.

John chose to ignore his inner voice and continued to travel further down a dead-end path that only led to his spiritual demise. No amount of counseling could change his mind.

When people begin the psychotherapy process, therapists simply guide their clients. We do not make decisions for them. People have to make their own choices.

I knew that John would continue to struggle with depression and that medication would only mask the symptoms as he continued to deny his own inner call for greater purpose in life. His spirit no longer was invested in his career because it was not authentically aligned with his higher self.

Depression is a natural consequence for not following your own inner voice.

The cost of ignoring or rejecting our authentic selves can have a determinantal long lasting impact on us emotionally, spiritually and physically. When we live a life that is not in alignment with our spirit, we pay a huge price.

People find ways of tuning out intuition when they know something to be right or wrong for them. When we ignore what is right for us, life will become heavier and denser as depression and unhappiness set in. The distress level may be slight at first, but after months or years, the distress can become unbearable and can have serious negative effects. What is calling us calls us for a reason.

♦

Jane, a fifty-three-year-old woman, works in a factory as a supervisor. She has worked for the same company for thirty years. Jane reports being happy in her current role up until about six months ago. She anguished over quitting her job and leaving, but due to her loyalty and benefits that she had accumulated, she resisted the urge to move on. Her intuition was guiding her to something better, something new, but her logical brain kept her stuck in a situation that she had outgrown.

"I used to love my job," Jane said forlornly as she stared out the window.

"Now I hate getting up in the morning and dread going in to work."

In therapy, we explored Jane's options. She could leave her current job and take her experience and knowledge into a new organization or completely new career, or she could stay and try to find other sources of happiness and meaning in everyday activities outside of work.

When life calls you to make a change, and it's time to move on, sometimes the energetic weight and inertia of not making changes takes away from other areas of life that do bring happiness.

I asked Jane what she dreamed of doing. Jane spoke with excitement about how she loved beer and would love to move to Colorado and work for a brewery giving tours. Jane has an outgoing and fun personality and I could clearly see her in this job role and enjoying the combination of socializing and talking about her passion and knowledge of beer.

We discussed pros and cons of Jane following her passion in relation to a career change. She got excited and enthusiastic about her future. She reported having a new-found sense of direction. Jane said she had a plan and informed me that she was moving forward.

Over the next several months, Jane continued psychotherapy. She decided that she was ready to start contacting brewing companies out west and was also looking for places to live. She left the session enthusiastic and hopeful.

Several months passed before I saw Jane again. I knew something was wrong the minute Jane walked into my office. She plopped herself down into a chair and said that she had discussed the move and relocation to Colorado with her husband and both were in agreement that the time wasn't right to move on.

Jane also reported that her depression symptoms had returned and said that her relationship with her coworkers and friends had deteriorated. She was also given more job responsibilities at work than ever before.

Jane now hated even more to get up in the mornings to go to work and no longer had energy to exercise or do the things that she previously enjoyed. Depression symptoms worsened as Jane's mental and physical health declined. She had forced herself to stay in a situation that no longer served her.

What Jane didn't understand was that it was her time to move on in life and until she acted on this, life would continue to get harder.

The old saying, when a door closes, another one opens up, is accurate in that if we trust that there is a greater reason for our discontentment and that we are not meant to stay in the same situation or same profession our entire lives. Then we open ourselves up to wonderful new opportunities or experiences that are aligned with a higher purpose.

It is not easy to take such a significant leap of faith; on the contrary, it may be the hardest thing you ever do, but the consequences of not following your own inner guidance, can be soul destroying.

LOSS OF SELF

Ann, a 49-year-old female client, and an administrator for a prominent university, reported having depression symptoms for over a decade. She was unfulfilled in her current role because it wasn't mentally or intellectually stimulating to her.

"Why do you stay in your job?" I asked her.

"For the benefits," Ann replied. "Most places don't give you snow days."

Ann stayed in the position for almost two decades. She was right: she needed her benefits because her job was making her ill. Symptoms included severe depression, lack of sleep and over-eating. Ann needed medication to stay in a job that depleted her spirit. As she lost interest in socializing and doing things outside of work, her energy levels plummeted, personally and professionally. Her health continued to decline along with her enthusiasm for life.

I asked Ann about her passions and her desires to be more creative and inspired in her work. Her energy shifted as her eyes lit up.

"I used to love teaching and working with foreign students. I would invite students over for dinner and have them cook meals from their home countries," she said with a smile.

"We had intellectual conversations about many different subjects, and I learned about each of their countries and the food was fantastic!"

Ann shared her passion for knowledge and mental stimulation. She wanted to be recognized at work for her intellectual and academic abilities, none of which were being fulfilled at the time.

Ann no longer believed that she would have other opportunities open up for her. What she didn't comprehend was that she needed to let go of what no longer served her. Ann remained in a dead-end job, believing that her career was the only source of her purpose in life.

Universally, something was shifting; the old path no longer led to fulfillment. The choice to stay in an organization that did not recognize her strengths leads to the decay of her spirit. Ann's doctor increased her depression medication, the only help available to keep her in a job that required all of her energy and strength to stay in it.

Ann's story was a traumatic one in that she was a gifted woman who had a lot to offer, but because of her fear of moving on, her gifts and strengths went unrecognized and unused. Her goals, her dreams, could not manifest because she hung onto what no longer served her higher purpose, and she no longer continued her search for meaning and was now too tired to find it in other areas of her life.

If we become unsettled or discontent with a job or relationship, it's usually because we are being guided to something better. I have experienced this first-hand in different situations in my life. I have held onto jobs that no longer served me for far too long. I understand why people don't move on in their lives, because the fear of the unknown can be terrifying. However, the price of not moving forward is by far too great.

In the past, I had accepted a job that I thought would be a good career move for me. It was closer to home and would reduce my daily commute of almost two hours.

Unfortunately, the job turned out to be toxic. The Director at the new job was anything but compassionate or caring, and often left employees feeling unsupported and unrecognized for their hard work. I didn't feel that this kind of environment supported me, yet my work required me to support people in need, people who required a lot of time, energy and attention. In fact, a significant number of clients that I worked with suffered from serious mental health issues.

It was only a few months into the job that I started to have health problems of my own. I found myself feeling exhausted, low in energy, and wanting to sleep at my desk. I had never felt so mentally and physically exhausted. I recognized the symptoms to be a sign that the position wasn't energetically right for me, yet I stayed for many of the same reasons that my clients did: the benefits.

As months passed, my health continued to deteriorate. Although I was a relatively healthy person, I had odd and unusual health issues including an out of the blue need for a root canal due to shooting pains in my head that brought me to my knees. I was also experiencing neck and jaw problems, and extreme exhaustion.

I remained in my job although my intuition was physically telling me that the job was making me ill. With a deteriorating physical condition, I discovered that the organization had cheated me out of a week's vacation pay. No one had informed me that vacation time had to be taken by a specific date. I thought time accrued and would roll over, but I was wrong. I had worked a full week without anyone informing me that I had earned time off. It was another significant sign or indication that I was in the wrong job.

I was furious with the organization for not informing me, but I was more upset with myself because my intuition had been screaming at me to get out; but I rationalized the decision and stayed. My health and finances took a toll.

Shortly after losing my vacation time, things got even worse. Feeling unappreciated for the hard work I was doing, I complained to friends and family, but I continued to go to work. Not being someone who calls in sick, I didn't take any sick days even though I was ill.

One day, I passed the Director in the hallway and said good morning to him, and he completely ignored me. That was the day I quit. I could not justify staying in a job where I was not acknowledged or recognized in any way.

Leaving that toxic environment behind, my health improved immediately. It was confirmation that the job was making me ill. I felt an immediate sense of relief.

Relationships

Sam, a middle-aged client, referred by his physician, began counseling for symptoms of depression. He lamented that he had been married for about thirty years and worked two jobs so that he didn't have to go home at night. He said his wife was an abusive alcoholic.

Over the years, the client had worked several jobs to avoid going home to his wife, but recently his second job had come to an end. Although he was retirement age, he continued to search for another job. I reminded him that home should be a place of nurturance and renewal.

"I hate going home," Sam nearly whispered. My wife is always drinking."

"Have you tried to get her help?" I asked.

"She doesn't want help. I don't know what else to do, but that's why I work so much. I hate being home with her," Sam said flatly.

The client participated in therapy for several months but was resistant to making changes. He expressed his feeling of hopelessness. I attempted to motivate the client to start bike riding after work as he expressed that biking was a passion of his. Sam had many excuses for not going. He had lost the will and desire to create any change.

I recognized at one point that I was working harder than the client to change his life. As Psychotherapists, we want people to succeed, and will often work harder than what clients are either willing or able to do. I sadly realized that this client felt that he was destined to spend the rest of his life in a toxic relationship with his wife.

Eventually Sam stopped coming to therapy even after weeks of trying to find ways to motivate him and help him find a greater purpose in his life. The toxicity of his marriage outweighed his desire to make changes. Relationships can often be a source of happiness or a source of pain. People sometimes stay in toxic relationships for far too long out of fear of the unknown, fear of being alone or fear of change.

The last time I saw Sam, his health had deteriorated, his wife continued to drink, and his doctor had increased his depression medication.

Sam's case is a traumatic example of how not changing or staying in the wrong place, in the wrong job, or with the wrong person, leads to the slow demise of the body, mind and spirit.

Making minor or major life changes is not easy. Saying goodbye to toxic people or to relationships that no longer serve us is difficult. Often times the familiar, even if dysfunctional, is more comfortable than facing the unknown. People often stay in abusive relationships because the fear of leaving is too great. That which is perceived as safety in staying with the familiar, outweighs the risk of leaving behind the toxic person or situation.

Another aspect of long-term relationships is that people often grow, and not always at the same time or in the same direction. The partner or spouse that does not grow feels threatened and struggles with the person who is changing. When two people grow in different directions, that may indicate that the relationship has outlived its purpose.

Other reasons people stay in unhealthy relationships is out of financial fear of not having the same income; yet, staying in situations too long takes a toll that sometimes can be irreversible. Being poor alone may be a temporary situation, compared with being better off financially but emotionally and spiritually depleted.

Sometimes people choose declining physical health over financial loss or a reduction in overall living expenses rather than making difficult decisions about their relationships.

Relationships are diverse and complex in nature and probably one of the biggest sources of personal happiness or unhappiness. Universally, we all seek to be understood, validated and loved unconditionally.

◆

Brad, a fifty-year-old client has been married to his wife for over thirty years. He had married his childhood sweetheart and because of his religion, felt compelled to stay married to her although he reported feeling unhappy and unfulfilled.

Brad no longer felt a connection to his wife, and said they often fought over money and finances. He had worked hard all of his life and had provided for his family, yet he quit his long-term job of twenty years simply because he no longer wanted to share his income with his wife. Brad was in the beginning stages of relationship denial.

"Why should I work to give her money?" Brad asked without wanting to hear an answer.

"Haven't you been supporting your wife for over thirty years?" I asked.

"Yes, but not anymore!" Brad said angrily.

Brad said that he felt "stuck" in his marriage, but divorce was not an option for him because of his religion.

Honoring and respecting Brad's decision to stay in his relationship, I worked with him on finding ways to create a stronger bond with his wife and encouraged them to engage in couple's therapy, but he resisted. Instead, he started to have fantasies about his female neighbor.

Whether or not Brad would change his mind and leave his wife was one thing. The answer, though, would not be found in another person, but in finding purpose and meaning in his current marriage, because he had made a vow to stay married and was making the decision to not divorce. When we make decisions, we need to ask ourselves if our choices will support us mentally, physically and spiritually.

In Brad's case, ending the marriage was not an option, so finding peace and working through issues would be necessary. He would also need to find other sources of purpose and meaning outside of the relationship. Sadly, Brad had chosen to not go to work anymore and refused couples counseling, narrowing his chances for happiness and for finding purpose and meaning in his life.

Marriages end and people change. Relationships can be complex and complicated, but when we choose to stay with someone, the reason we stay will determine the experience we have.

If we are dedicated to staying in the relationship, then the willingness to work through issues is critical. However, if the relationship is abusive or toxic then underlying issues within the relationship also need to be explored. If abuse is involved, then leaving would be recommended. No one should endure an abusive relationship of any kind. Abuse depletes self-esteem, self-worth, identity and happiness.

The reasons people stay in bad relationships vary. Issues can and should be worked through if wanted, but there are relationships that are so toxic that neither person can remain healthy.

Recognizing if a relationship has outgrown its course or if it needs healing can be difficult to decipher.

Sometimes there is purpose and meaning being in an unhappy relationship in that it may allow us the spiritual lesson of growth, although usually in a difficult or painful fashion.

Over the years, I have heard hundreds of reasons why people stay in toxic relationships. Again, fear of leaving and the unknown are common. People will also stay in hopes that they can change the other person. We cannot change others: people have to be willing to change. The only person we can change is ourselves.

Personal growth is often associated with the quality of our relationships.

We learn the most about ourselves through our relationships with others. Other people cannot make us happy. Happiness is our responsibility, but people, the right people, can assist us on the road to personal happiness, purpose and meaning.

How does your relationship make you feel? Are you growing alone or together? If you are alone and not in a personal relationship, how do you find purpose and meaning being single? On this earth journey, we will all be alone at some point. But whether parts of that journey are alone or shared, there is always meaning in the journey.

Ask yourself a series of questions. Does the relationship support you? Does the relationship foster growth? Do you feel valued? Do you enjoy being together? If the answer is no to any of these questions, then ask yourself: why are you in the relationship? How can you make it healthier and happier? What is the purpose for staying? What is the purpose for leaving? There are always lessons of personal growth to be found.

◆

Nancy, a fifty-eight-year-old client described ongoing conflict with her sister. She said her sister would get angry at her for no reason and would stop talking to her. Nancy, a strong communicator, would try to work through issues related to her sister's anger, but her sister would give her the silent treatment and not communicate why she was angry. She would cut her off, leaving Nancy feeling sad, frustrated and alone.

Nancy was frustrated attempting to talk to her sister about her feelings over the years with no positive results. Nancy found herself in a pattern of emotional abandonment. She had spent her entire life trying to strengthen the relationship with her sister, but through the therapy process, she was able to identify an unhealthy dysfunctional pattern that continued long into adulthood.

"When I least expect it, Stacy will start an argument with me," Nancy said.

"I am usually aware of what she is trying to do, and I try not to get drawn in, then she gets nastier and eventually says something really mean. I end up getting angry and will try to redirect the conversation, but she hangs up and stops talking to me!" Nancy said in frustration.

Nancy was the victim of her sister's own unresolved anger. Her sister found Nancy to be an easy target when she felt angry or upset and would take it out on Nancy, who never knew when she would be abruptly cut off or cut out of her sister's life.

Nancy reported that in the past, her sister had stopped talking to her for years, although she had reached out in numerous attempts to work things out. Regardless, her sister was unable and unwilling to do so.

After three years of silence, Nancy's sister emailed and wanted to connect again. Nancy missed her sister and engaged in a relationship with her, only to be cut out of her life once again.

Nancy was able to express that, reflecting back, she saw a lifetime pattern of dysfunctional communication. In therapy, she expressed her sadness and also said that she did not know if having a relationship with her sister would benefit her anymore. She was tired of feeling sad, unheard and disrespected.

Nancy's choice was to cease communication with her sister, knowing that at some point in the future, her sister would contact her. Next time, however, she would not allow her sister back into her life. Nancy's decision to move on from a toxic family relationship was a difficult one. She accepted that her sister may never change, and she decided that she no longer needed to place herself in the role of victim.

Through the therapy process, Nancy worked on grief and loss. She mourned the loss of her sister, the one that she had shared many happy times with, in the past. She grieved the pain and moved on.

Nancy accepted that she could not change her sister or her dysfunctional patterns. The only thing she could do was to protect herself and build healthier and happier relationships with other people.

Nancy finally came to a place of acceptance and healing. She let go and moved on in life, recognizing self-respect and healthy boundaries as essential in her search for meaning and purpose.

The decision to not be involved with family members is one of the hardest decisions a person can make but is sometimes a necessary one.

Ideally, family is supposed to be supportive and nurturing, but sometimes family can be the source of extreme pain. Finding purpose and meaning in all relationships is the key to greater fulfillment and personal self-growth.

Anger

Daniel, a forty-three-year-old client, an ex-convict, wanted to seek revenge on his ex-wife because she neglected to drive him to his court hearing. He wanted to force a paternity test to prove that he was not the father to his son that he had supported for the past 13 years.

"I'm going to throw the paternity papers at the boy," Daniel said angrily.

"Do you mean your son?" I enquired.

"Yes," he said through gritted teeth.

When pointing out that his son was the victim in all of this, he becomes angry and insisted that he was the victim. He went on to say that he didn't care who he hurt. He was told to care.

Daniel later broke his probation, left the halfway house that he was living in, and now had a warrant out for his arrest.

Anger and hatred create a toxicity in the body like no other toxin. Holding onto anger is a choice that depletes happiness and inner peace.

Daniel didn't care who he hurt. He was incapable of understanding that even if he was not the biological father to his son, he was the only father the boy had ever known. The client only cared about himself and would stop at nothing to try and gain power over the situation. His anger and hatred were the driving forces that would cloud his judgement and create a life less lived.

When people become wounded, they sometimes go into a place of no return. Anger clouds reason and judgement and generates negative stories of fantasy. The energy of anger is powerful in that the end results are destruction to the body, mind, and spirit.

Anger in the body creates stress and tension, increased blood pressure, stiff muscles, clenched jaw, and tension headaches.

In the mind, anger creates a darkness that consumes negative thinking patterns. The person stuck in anger cannot see anything else but their own pain and suffering; they become oblivious to any lessons learned from the situation as they only focus on the negative in their lives.

In psychotherapy I have heard thousands of personal stories of anger including stories involving relationship betrayals, loss of jobs or redundancy, being the victim of physical or sexual abuse, and murder.

Anger is a secondary emotion. Underlying anger is always sadness. However, for many, anger is easier to express. Feeling sad is often portrayed as a sign of weakness, but we need to remember that crying is healthy. Unresolved anger becomes toxic and has been linked to many physical ailments and diseases.

Emotions are forms of energy. As an energy, anger carries a heaviness that takes a toll spiritually, mentally, and physically in a destructive and ruthless way. People who get stuck in anger tend to use maladaptive coping skills such as using drugs or alcohol, or other forms of negative ways to numb their feelings.

What is the purpose of anger? Anger, or feeling victimized can be difficult to shift out of, especially if you feel you have been wronged. In therapy, people struggle with feeling that their lives have been derailed and have difficulty finding purpose and meaning after being victimized. There is always a lesson in anger.

Being willing to undergo sometimes painful therapeutic processes in which you have to release pain, enter a healing stage, and acknowledge the strengths that you gained from the experience is necessary work that results in a greater sense of personal purpose and meaning. Although hanging onto anger is always a choice, it is never a happy one.

◆

Debbie a twenty-eight-year-old female client began the counseling process to work through grief and loss. Her mother had been brutally murdered by her husband. Debbie was grief stricken and angry.

"Why did this happen to me? Why my mother?" Debbie asked grabbing Kleenex from the box.

Understandably she had been robbed of her mother, and although the incident had taken place years earlier, she was still angry. Remember that underlying anger is always sadness.

Over time, Debbie was able to process her feelings and turn her anger into a self-empowering lesson in which she became an activist for women nationwide by speaking about domestic violence and making a positive purpose out of her mother's senseless murder.

Debbie struggled for years trying to find purpose and meaning in her life after her mother's death, but she eventually was able to heal and accept that she now had a new purpose, in spite of, or because of, a tragic and life shattering experience.

Randy, a well-dressed businessman, a thirty-nine-year-old client, arrived at my office for counseling. He reported that he was recently released from prison where he had spent eight years for embezzlement. Randy had been charged for stealing money from his father's business. Randy's brother had reported him to the authorities.

After an investigation and court trial, he was found guilty of embezzlement and sentenced to prison, where he learned more criminal behaviors. Randy began using women on the outside for money and material items and setting up false senses of relationships unbeknown to the women involved.

Randy verbally purged his life story to me, and explained that when he was a child, he could not do anything to please his father no matter how hard he tried. His father favored and praised his older brother while verbally and physically abusing him. Yet, Randy continued to try to gain his father's approval and validation.

Then one day things changed. The client described an incident in which he was sent to the store to purchase a can of corn for dinner. The client found a different brand than what his father had asked him to get but decided to purchase it anyway because it was on sale.

Randy excitedly ran home believing his father would be proud of him for saving money.

Back home, Randy proudly showed his father the can of corn and the extra money he had saved, but instead of being happy, his father was outraged and began to physically beat him.

"Something changed in me at that moment," Randy said with a cold, blank look in his eyes.

"What do you mean?" I asked.

"Something snapped inside of me. I knew at that moment, I would never let anyone ever hurt me again," he said coldly.

Later in life, Randy went on to victimize people in numerous ways. He was harming others to get back at his father for a childhood of emotional and physical abuse.

Numerous people likely searched for understanding and for purpose in meaning for reasons why they were victimized by Randy. The destructive pattern continued.

The client began the therapy process, not to work through underlying pain or abuse, but because his employer had accused him of sexual harassment, and he was again facing legal charges. Randy denied the accusations and later claimed that he was actually the victim of sexual harassment. Randy wanted to start legal actions against his employer, a large, well-known organization. He wanted his false accusations documented in therapy. Randy's only motive was to protect himself.

Several attempts were made to help the client understand that his behaviors were connected to his father's inability to recognize or value him as a child, but the client was resistant to change.

Most people experience anger at different levels and to different degrees. Anger is a healthy emotion if it is acknowledged, processed and released, but left unresolved, it becomes destructive and toxic to the self and others.

Sometimes people become addicted to being angry and find reasons to stay mad, picking fights or arguments with others or making themselves the victim in situations. People sometimes find power in anger and spend lifetimes stuck with destructive and toxic emotions.

◆

Justin, a sixteen-year-old adolescent male was court ordered into residential treatment for sexually abusing his younger sibling.

Halfway through the therapy process, Justin disclosed that his mother had remarried, and his stepfather had been abusing him. He had told several teachers at school and a Child Protective Services (CPS) investigation was performed, which resulted in a ruling out of abuse. That result left Justin in the home with mother, sister and stepfather, the abuser.

"My mother saw my stepfather beating me and did nothing," Justin said with tears in his eyes. "She just watched."

Silence filled the office as Justin reflected on what he felt was his mother's emotional abandonment and failure to protect and defend him.

After telling several people who were mandated reporters about the abuse, Justin expressed in therapy that he made the decision to sexually abuse his sister because he knew that would result in him being removed from his home.

Justin's story was tragic. No one had protected him, so he believed that the only way to save himself and to get away from his abuser was to become an abuser and to abuse his own sister.

Justin's plan worked. He was removed from his home and placed into residential treatment.

Justin was able to work through his anger and underlying sadness in regard to both his mother and stepfather. He completed sexual offender-specific treatment and was eventually released.

In this case, Justin was in search of safety and validation. He was also in search of meaning to a life of abuse, both as a victim as well as coming to terms with his own abuse of his sibling. I also knew that he would need to reflect on his abusive behaviors several times throughout his life and continue to release anger to heal himself. He would also have to work on healing his relationship with his sister, if that was even possible.

Anger is an interesting emotion in that it can alter clarity and direction in life. Anger can change motives. And if left unresolved, can prevent clarity of finding or achieving purpose and meaning in life.

Health and Wellness

Kathy, a fifty-year-old female client created dolls with distinct personalities that came alive in her mind, to distract herself from an empty, joyless marriage.

Kathy developed COPD, Chronic Obstructive Pulmonary Disease, that prevented her from breathing easily. After years of repressed anger, she was suffocating symbolically and physically. Not willing to move on or end the relationship, Kathy developed more health problems in the years to follow. Her body was talking to her, yet she did not listen to those warning signs.

In the past, body, mind and spirit were not considered to be related, but today we know that all systems are interconnected. We cannot alter one system without affecting another.

Is there purpose and meaning in illness? Illness is a powerful teacher and can lead us in directions that we may not seek otherwise. Sickness or disease can be a drastic call to change life directions or paths, whether it be in one's career, relationships or overall health maintenance.

No one chooses sickness over health, but when we have an ailment, we need to search for an underlying root cause. Something needs to change. It could be work, relationships or health. In some cases, it could be in all of those areas.

A friend once asked me for advice about a health problem they were having. I said if you go to a doctor, they will prescribe medication and give you a physical diagnosis and treat your body. If you go to a Psychologist or Licensed Professional Counselor, they will give you a mental health diagnosis and treat your mind. Sometimes people deny that their issues are psychological or physical because that would require change and change can be one of the most difficult things for people to do, even when we know it's good for us.

Until there is an illness, we usually take health for granted.

In psychotherapy, physical illness can be linked to other issues including mental health. Our bodies are a major source of wisdom and they intuitively know what foods are good for us and what foods are bad. Our bodies are always speaking to us, but it's easy to ignore those messages when we have a sugar or caffeine addiction, for example. Giving up a beloved food or drink is difficult, but when it starts to impact your physical and mental health, the symptoms can be severe.

For several years, unexpectedly, I experienced health issues. I started to suffer from migraines, my asthma worsened, caffeine caused eye flashers, and sugar caused me to feel exhausted and irritable. I continued to suffer and went to several doctors asking if it was something that I was eating or ingesting that was making me ill. Diet and nutrition were quickly dismissed, leaving me to suffer for almost two years before a severe allergy to dairy products was diagnosed.

I had also developed several food intolerances. My body no longer tolerated certain foods, and they were foods that I loved, even craved. I began a long-term process of cutting out the bad foods and found the process difficult.

Was there a purpose to me developing food allergies? At first, I thought no, that it was senseless and had no meaning other than to deprive me of what I loved.

I eventually learned that there was purpose in my developing food allergies. I would later go on to recognize how food is medicine and how food has a direct impact on mental health and overall physical health. I also later became a Certified Mental Health Integrated Medicine Provider, helping people to examine their diet in relation to overall health and wellness.

Therefore, what I thought was a horrible forced life change, was actually positive because it later led me into a new direction that I would not have otherwise taken.

Grief and Loss

Julia, an elderly female client, was grieving the loss of her adult son who died unexpectedly. After only a few months, her friends told her she needed to see a doctor for depression. She went to her doctor who prescribed antidepressants. Although she reported grieving the loss of her son, she remained on medication for years. When she later stopped taking the medication, her sadness returned. She still had unresolved grief that she had never worked through. The medication had masked her emotions and halted the natural grieving process. When she started to feel the loss of her son again, she went back to her doctor who instructed her to continue with the antidepressants.

"My friends said I needed to see my doctor to get help because I was crying all the time," she said.

"But you are going through the grieving process," I responded. "You lost your only son. It's natural to be crying. You are experiencing one of the hardest things a mother could ever go through," I said, trying to help Julia understand that the grieving process takes time.

Until Julia was willing to acknowledge the pain and grief of her son's passing, she would continue to take medication and repress her emotions.

Depression always has a root cause that might be based in several causes. Although it is painful to work through those causes, it is essential to the healing process. We are not meant to live a life of woundedness, but of wholeness, and happiness.

Visions

Danny, a middle-aged male client disclosed shooting himself in the face three years earlier.

"I had a vision in which Red Cloud told me to go to San Francisco," Danny said.

"Please tell me more about your vision," I responded.

"Red Cloud told me to get rid of everything, so I gave away my car and all of my belongings and traveled to California," Danny said softly. "But I ended up in a psychiatric hospital."

Immediately after discharge, Danny traveled back to Wisconsin and shot himself again, this time in the head. He survived the suicide attempt and was left with facial scars and a tracheotomy. He talked about recurrent visions of death.

Somewhere, somehow, Danny had lost his spirit and desire to live.

Danny's story is one of the hardest series of therapy sessions I have ever experienced.

Together we explored everyday life and what held purpose and meaning for Danny that could help him get through the day. He shared memories of the past in which he would forage for food, including berries, asparagus and mushrooms.

Through simple, yet personal meaningful activities, Danny began to find purpose in his life again. He no longer talked about dying but shared his excitement about going into the woods and finding food that he once loved to collect. He also started a morning routine of getting up to watch the sunrise, giving thanks for the new day.

Danny struggled with serious mental health issues, yet with help and guidance, he was able to find purpose and meaning in everyday living while working toward both long term and short-term goals.

Purpose is found in the present moment.

Trauma

Beth, an elderly female client processed her emotions through decoupaging pieces of furniture around her small apartment. Each item represented some kind of trauma she had experienced as a child and adult. Beth's house was a museum of a lifetime of trauma.

"Instead of crying, I decoupage," Beth stated. "Do you want to see pictures of my apartment?" she said holding out a photo album.

Trauma and abuse can be the hardest to heal in that the level of abuse can be soul destroying.

Clients often get stuck in abuse and find it difficult to move forward. The search for understanding abuse or reasons for it, can last a lifetime, often without any answers.

Abuse is never easy to work through; it is complex and complicated on many levels, and each healing journey is unique. It is my role to assist people in their search to find lost parts of their spirit.

Abuse can have negative physical affects. I often see a significant recovery in physical symptoms when emotional pain begins to heal.

People who have been the victim of abuse often feel their lives lack meaning or direction. Trauma can lead to a complete breakdown of the spirit, in which that has been lost, needs to be found again.

Psychotherapy can be a difficult and painful journey, but it is through healing that personal strengths can be developed and acknowledged.

Beth used her creativity as a way to heal and work through a painful childhood that had left her emotionally scarred. Once she began the process of healing, her physical symptoms began to improve and she started attending a crafting circle, sharing her passion for creative arts with others. Beth found a greater sense of purpose in her life as she shared a connection with others.

Is there purpose and meaning to be found in trauma? The answer to this question varies depending on who you ask. Abuse is not acceptable in any form, but when someone has been victimized, it's important that they identify and discover the strengths that helped them to survive.

In the profession of Mental Health and Substance Abuse, some of the best therapists have been the victims of abuse or have struggled with addiction problems. Through their own experiences, they found their life's purpose in helping others on the same journey.

Life is full of lessons, some of them lead us away from our purpose and some of them lead us to our purpose.

SPIRITUALITY

Mary, a thirty-seven-year-old female client and a victim of long-term domestic violence went to New Mexico and had a spiritual experience where the mountains played beautiful music to her.

Her life shifted as she no longer settled for a life less lived. New experiences and opportunities opened up to her as she pushed herself out of her comfort zone.

People have searched for purpose and meaning for thousands of years. The search for meaning can take many different paths, yet it all leads back to the self.

The search for spiritual meaning can take people through the dark night of the soul. This can be experienced on many levels, and in different ways.

The dark night of the soul can be a difficult and painful experience, as life as we know it, no longer serves us and we no longer feel called to a greater purpose.

During this process, what once held meaning to us, no longer does and we struggle to see a way forward.

People from all walks of life, ages, and backgrounds go through the dark night of the soul and for many that path leads nowhere.

It is during these searches that it is necessary to let go and trust that something else will open up. This doesn't mean sitting back and doing nothing. When you least feel like it, you may need to work the hardest.

◆

Amy, a forty-six-year-old female client who lost her husband through illness, was forced to move out of their family home. She also had to caretake for her mother who had dementia. She began the therapy process working through grief and loss in relation to her husband's death, the loss of her home, and her mother's ongoing memory loss.

Amy questioned why all of these tragic things had happened to her. Of course, there were no answers, but together in therapy we worked on finding purpose in everyday life, especially with her mother as with dementia, every moment mattered.

"I lose patience with my mom and then I feel so guilty," Amy said picking at her fingernails. "I work all day and then come home and have more work to do. I'm tired and exhausted and although I understand she needs help, I'm burned out."

Amy's new and current role of caregiver was not one that she wanted or would have chosen, but in life, she had been placed in this position and through the therapeutic process, we discussed how this role could have purpose and meaning for her in ways that she could not yet see.

Amy struggled to be a patient caregiver to her mother but started to be mindful of their time together and made the most out of it. During this process, she questioned and cried and felt that life had handed her a raw deal, but over time she was able to find purpose in taking care of her mother. She joined a support group and began to help other people who were in the same situation. She downsized her home and found purpose in living small. Amy began to minimize her living costs, met others who were interested in Eco Living and a whole new way of life opened up for her.

It was not an easy process for Amy, but eventually she came to understand that the old way of living had ended, and a new way of life had begun.

When experiencing the dark night of the soul, it's important to stay hopeful and continue one's search. One must trust that there is purpose in everything you experience.

One of my favorite poems by Emerson reads:

"Life is but a mutable cloud, forever and always changing."

As we continue our search for meaning, we will always endure physical, mental, emotional and spiritual hardships. Even in the darkest of nights, if you continue to search, a new path will be found.

ADDICTION

Mark, a thirteen-year-old adolescent male client repeatedly huffed gasoline until he had permanent brain damage. He abused substances as a means to escape physical and emotional abuse.

"Huffing made me numb," Mark said in group therapy. "It helped me to forget all the shit that I went through."

Mark tried to piece together his painful past as he had now been court- ordered into residential treatment. Not able to fully comprehend the extent of the damage that huffing caused, he tried to piece together his life and what it meant.

◆

Barb, a sixty-three-year-old professional woman, questioning drinking a bottle of wine every night and if she had an alcohol problem.

Barb said she began drinking at an early age. She also reported that when her parents were working, as a child, it was her responsibility to take care of her siblings. She had to cook the meals, clean the house, and be the full-time parent.

"It wasn't right," Barb reflected. "I was just a kid. I wanted to play and do things that other kids my age were doing, but instead I was cooking and cleaning and taking care of my brothers and sisters. I hate my parents for that."

As an adolescent, Barb rebelled and started drinking alcohol which helped to repress the deep-seated anger that she had toward her parents and siblings.

As a child, Barb was more than one hundred pounds overweight. At the age of 10, Barb had been placed on medication, stimulants, by her doctor and due to her weight issues, she was bullied and picked on by other children.

Barb found that drinking helped to relieve the sadness and anger and continued long into adulthood as she relied on alcohol as a maladaptive coping skill.

Due to the addiction and consumption of alcohol, Barb remained stuck in an unhealthy pattern of anger, not being able to move forward or to stop the addiction; therefore, she did not find purpose and meaning in her life.

Barb continued to drink and remained in denial that she was an alcoholic. Her relationships with her husband, children and siblings deteriorated as she traveled further into her addiction.

People use or abuse substances for many reasons, and there is always an underlying reason.

Addictions come in all forms ranging from alcohol, drugs, overeating, gambling, shopping, and gaming. Anything can become an addiction and addictions prevent people from finding purpose and meaning.

Addictions can be one of the most significant blockages to finding direction in life. They keep people stuck in negative energy patterns that prevent life from moving forward. Until the addiction is acknowledged, worked through, and released, nothing moves forward.

Addictions are the root cause for the loss of self in that they prevent the authentic self from emerging.

Some of the hardest cases I have worked with involve people with a lifetime of addictions. For them, their purpose becomes feeding the addiction and keeping it alive. The addiction overshadows the search for purpose and meaning in that it consumes the body, mind and soul.

Addictions need to be acknowledged, understood, processed, healed and released and then greater purpose in the areas of life paths and life purposes will be unveiled.

VALIDATION

Josh, an 11-year-old boy sat outside school waiting for a ride. As I walked past him to my car carrying ceramic windchimes from a 5th grade art class, he said, "I made one of those."

I asked him which one he made, and he quickly identified it and said he wrote a poem about it.

I asked him to tell me about the poem. Josh started to tell me about his prior home where he played by a nearby pond.

Josh appeared melancholy. I asked him, "Do you live in town now?"

"Yes, my mom lives over there," he said pointing his finger, "And I live over there," he said pointing his finger in the opposite direction.

Josh's parents had obviously divorced and he had been forced to move from a home that he loved.

I said, "Maybe one day you will once again live in a house near a pond."

As I drove away, I thought about Josh and wondered if his parents had any idea that he missed his home or if they ever took the time to find out what he was thinking or feeling.

Josh carried a sense of aloneness and needed validation for his feelings of loss. He needed to tell someone about his pain. He did not know I was a therapist; he simply shared his feelings with a stranger. I listened to what he said and acknowledged his feelings in the hope that this would help start the healing process for him.

We all need validation in life for different events that we have experienced. We also need to be heard.

Until authentic validation occurs, we struggle to find meaning in that we matter. Many people do not get validated in childhood and search for validation their entire lives. In this case, we have no choice but to validate ourselves and to learn how to hear our own inner voice and calling.

LIFE TRANSITIONS

Jacki, a fifty-year-old female client arrived at her first therapy session in a wheelchair.

"My life changed one day when a young woman driver hit my car. I was left paralyzed on my left side," Jacki said sadly.

Ten years later, she was facing the possibility of losing her leg due to ongoing infections.

I listened as Jacki shared her story. Six years earlier, she had been in a coma for three months when the medical team encouraged her husband to take her off of life support. He refused. Soon after that, she came out of the coma.

"I saw my deceased mother when I was in the hospital," Jacki said softly.

"She told me it was not yet my time to pass over."

When Jacki had recovered, she wondered why it was not yet her time and why she would have to live the rest of her life in a wheelchair. Jacki struggled with depression and felt her life had no meaning.

Jacki continued to talk about her boredom in daily life being confined to a wheelchair. Together, we worked on creating a new life plan, one that began with finding purpose and meaning in each day.

For years, Jacki struggled to understand why the accident had happened to her. Eventually she was able to change her focus, accepting that there were no answers, but by letting go and releasing the trauma, she was able to shift into finding a new purpose in life. She started to find new passions and new interests that she never had before.

Life can bring unwanted experiences in the areas of relationships, career and home. People die or leave us. Our careers come to an end or we retire. Our homes are broken into, flooded or burned down, or we are faced with having to move, resize or relocate.

I have worked with numerous clients going through major life changes. Most of the time, the changes are not welcomed or initiated, but usually forced upon us as we kick and scream trying to keep things the same.

Life never stays the same; it's always changing although at times it seems to be redundant when we are seeking or desiring change and transition. Life is a paradox.

Through my own experiences, I know that when life becomes unsettled, it's a warning sign that unless you make changes, things often get worse. I have worked with clients who have had red flags that life is trying to shift them into new experiences, but they want to hang onto the old and the familiar because the fear of the unknown is scary. But what is even scarier is living a life of stagnation, where nothing changes, and everything stays the same. That stagnation only results in the slow demise of the soul.

It is through new experiences that we grow the most. By moving through fear, we find strengths we didn't know we had. Our lives open up and our world expands.

Throughout our journeys we may need to release people that we have traveled with in the past. Their part of the journey may be over with as the next passenger, or guide, may be waiting just down the road. If you refuse to stop the car and let the old passenger out, the new passenger who brings new experiences, new opportunities and new growth, cannot get in, and remains unknown.

Life is meant to be shared.

◆

Tina, a middle-aged female client, came to my office one day as a referral from another counselor to work through career changes. My colleague knew that I enjoyed helping people through significant life transitions.

Tina had been a teacher for over twenty years, but she no longer felt joy or passion in her career and struggled with depression.

"If you could do anything, what would you do?" I asked.

"I used to love flowers and working in the nursery when I was in college. This may sound silly, but I used to dream about owning a floral shop. Being around plants and flowers always made me happy," Tina said.

"What keeps you from living your dream now?" I asked.

"It's too late now. I have invested too much time in my profession to leave now and start again," Tina said defensively.

We are not always destined to work in one career our entire lifetime. Although some people can be happy staying in one career for thirty or more years, new opportunities, new learning experiences and new people can be found and create positive change.

Tom, a twenty-eight-year-old male client began psychotherapy reporting that he had been incarcerated for about five years. I patiently listened as he outlined the different charges that caused him to be locked up. He then expressed an interest and desire to change is life.

"I learned how to meditate in prison. It changed my life," he said proudly.

"How did it help you?" I asked.

"It brought me freedom," he said.

"In what way? Can you explain more?" I asked.

"I was locked up, but through meditation, my mind was free, and I could go anywhere. It made me interested in how our thoughts are energy and how we can change and transform them. I tested it out in prison, and it works!" Tom said with a smile on his face.

Tom's interest in energy psychology surprised me. Together we explored alternative therapies including energy psychology and advanced mindfulness.

Tom was making huge life changes in every area of his life.

When the decision to change is made, the universe almost always tests you. Tom was tested immediately. We worked through those tests in therapy, which could have resulted in relapse and criminal behaviors; however, he recognized the tests and the challenges and stayed strong.

Life opened up for Tom in ways that he could never have imagined. He was offered several jobs and was promoted to supervisor. He moved into better housing and started to volunteer at organizations that made him feel good about himself.

Tom's willingness and hard work to create a better life had significant results. Although he had a past criminal history, he did not become a victim of it and did not let that past limit his life in any way. He made the choice to find purpose and meaning and verbalized a desire to help others.

Tom's life progressed at an alarming rate as he released his past and found purpose on a new road.

It wasn't easy for Tom as he sometimes struggled with unexpected difficulties, but he continued his practice of self-care, daily meditation, and a healthy diet.

No matter what your past, you can find purpose in your journey. Accept where you are, where you came from and find peace and purpose in the moment.

STRESS

Hailey, a twenty-eight-year-old professional client, was referred to counseling by her doctor for symptoms of anxiety and depression.

Hailey weighed over 300 pounds and suffered from insomnia and rosacea. She wept as she shared that over the previous year, she quit her job in the medical field and had gained over 100 pounds, was forced to move into low income housing, broke up with her fiancé, and her son had been kicked out of school.

The client reported that she was emotional eating to deal with the stress, which further exacerbated her depression symptoms. Her son's aggressive behavioral problems had stopped her from working because school would only allow him to attend two hours daily.

Due to all the stress, Hailey developed anxiety symptoms and struggled to feel good about herself, her son, or her future.

Within a year, Hailey had lost a meaningful career, her family, her home, her relationship and her physical health.

Life was forcing unwanted and unexpected changes. With help from her doctor, Hailey began to engage in therapy.

"My entire life is ruined," Hailey said, wiping tears from her face. "I had a great job, a nice house and a fiancé. Now I have nothing."

Together we worked on core issues of depression and anxiety. Hailey felt depressed because of her life circumstances, the loss of her job, her excessive weight gain, and her son's behavioral problems. She had been prescribed medication by her doctor yet continued to feel depressed and had panic attacks daily.

We began by looking at things that brought joy and passion to Hailey's life. She shared that she loved working on creative projects and in the past, had made her own aromatherapy soaps and lotions. Hailey was encouraged to use this time at home to reconnect with her passions.

Hailey set up a working space in the basement of her home and began to make beautiful aromatic soaps that she started to sell at the local farmer's market. Hailey started to find purpose in an old hobby.

Together, we addressed weight issues and feelings of low self-esteem. The client expressed a desire to eat raw, healthy foods and had an interest in making her own sauces, smoothies and dips. Again, she was encouraged to follow her passion. She planted a vegetable garden and began to create healthy foods for her entire family.

After several months of counseling, Hailey stopped coming in for therapy. In psychotherapy, it's not unusual for a client to stop coming in when they have made progress or feel better, as they no longer feel the need for therapy. Although I wondered how Hailey was doing, I assumed that if she needed me, she would reach out.

Over a year had passed when I saw Hailey's name back on my list for scheduled appointments. I walked out into the crowded waiting room and called her name. I was shocked when a beautiful, thin, young woman approached me with a huge smile on her face. She said, "Hello!"

I was shocked. I couldn't believe this was the same client that I had seen a year earlier. She had lost over 100 pounds, her skin looked radiant, and she was smiling ear to ear. I had never seen such a dramatic change or transformation.

Hailey followed me to my office and sat down on the couch. She proudly told me about how she had changed her life and how happy she was. She explained that her entire transformation resulted in a simple change. She stopped eating junk food and ate only organic, plant-based, raw foods.

Hailey reported that she had always had an interest in eating raw and started making homemade sauces, dips, soups and smoothies and consumed protein through nuts and lentils.

Hailey's entire life transformed. She had lost over 100 pounds, the depression and anxiety symptoms were gone, and she no longer took medication. She felt better, she looked great, her energy levels returned, and she had gone back to work.

Not only did Hailey's personal and professional life change, but her son, who also consumed the same raw natural diet, was able to go back to school with a significant improvement in behavior.

Hailey showed up at my office again another year later. She had lost even more weight, reported that she was dating again and had traveled to South America to volunteer her medical expertise and had met the love of her life. She continued to eat raw healthy foods and felt energized, clarity of mind and improved sleep. The anxiety and depression symptoms did not return. None of the prescribed medication had helped, but her change in diet was the catalyst for significant change.

There is a significant link between food and mood. People often reject that food has such impact in their lives, but it can have amazing results.

Sometimes the answers we seek for purpose come through our physical bodies. In Hailey's case, her entire life had broken down. Through this difficult experience, she not only rediscovered her old passions, but she discovered new ones. Hailey's entire life had transformed.

◆

Sarah, a twenty-nine-year-old female client, began psychotherapy for ongoing physical alignments for which she had endured numerous medical procedures. Untreated migraines were an ongoing problem that often resulted in Sarah spending days in bed, unable to work.

Sarah reported having a young child that she was unable to care for. Her husband did most of the caretaking, cooking and cleaning.

"I can't play with my daughter anymore, Sarah said. She usually sits in bed with me when I have migraines, which is almost every day. I feel like a bad mother, but nothing has helped me."

I worked with Sarah on identifying issues associated with her migraines and underlying feelings associated with illness. Unresolved emotions can create physical and somatic symptoms.

Sarah expressed her ongoing relationship conflict with her mother. Her illnesses began in childhood and it was through sickness that her mother would be kind and nurturing toward her; otherwise, her mother had no time for her. As a child, Sarah had learned that illness resulted in being cared for.

Working through Sarah's unmet needs, she started to feel better emotionally and physically.

We began to discuss food and nutrition, but Sarah was resistant to changing her diet and quickly declined making any dietary changes, even if they were making her ill.

It appeared, however, that some of her migraines and other health related issues were caused by a poor diet.

In therapy, I shared my own personal experience with food in hopes that it would motivate Sarah to start an elimination diet to see if the foods she was consuming were the root cause of her health problems, but as a therapist, all I can do is make recommendations. I never tell people what to do or make choices for them.

Sarah quickly dismissed and rejected that the foods she ate had anything to do with her health issues. I continued to encourage her to at least try to keep a food diary; however, changing her diet was not something that she wanted to do. Sarah would rather suffer than give up some of her favorite foods which were likely causing her to gain weight and have migraines.

Sometimes simple changes in diet can change your life for the better. We are conditioned to seek help through medication for all types of emotional and physical alignments when food is often the culprit.

I personally learned the connection between food and mood several years ago when I began to have recurrent health issues.

Over a two-year period, I sought medical help to determine the causes of worsening asthma and migraines. I intuitively knew the answer but did not want to accept it. I asked various doctors if the food I was eating could possibly be causing my symptoms, but was consistently told, "No".

Eventually, a nurse practitioner ordered lab work, which confirmed that I had developed a serious dairy allergy. Dairy had been something I had eaten my entire life. I loved it, but my body was rejecting it and causing me to get ill.

Once I stopped eating dairy, my asthma stopped, and my migraines ceased. I felt better in a short period of time. It was not easy to give up foods I loved.

At the same time, I also developed an intolerance for caffeine and chocolate. I had to give up cheese, milk, yogurt, coffee and chocolate. Several people would remark to me that they would rather die than give up their coffee or cheese. I thought, how foolish.

When clients come to me with depression or anxiety, I question them about their diets. I hear about unhealthy eating habits and most people quickly dismiss the idea that food can be making them sick or depressed.

Over the years, my mind reflects back to the client whose life changed dramatically, simply because she changed her diet.

KINDNESS

I lived in Southern England for twelve years and toward the end, I experienced a very difficult period in my life in which my life changed drastically.

My home, my family, and my foundation crumbled, and I was in the midst of creating a new life for myself.

This was one of the darkest times in my life. I remember taking the Underground train to the center of London to meet with a financial advisor. The situation was bleak, and I couldn't see any happy endings at the time.

My train had reached the "the end of line," but I sat in oblivion, unaware that the train had stopped or that it was actually underground, and that people were exiting the carriage.

As I sat there staring out the window in silence, lost in a state of hopelessness, I noticed the man who had been sitting across from me, exit the train to return moments later. He walked up to me and said, "Miss the train has stopped. It's not going any further. You must get off."

"Thank you," I said as I stood up and walked out of the carriage in a fog.

Somehow this stranger, who did not know me, was aware of my suffering and took the time to come back to let me know that my journey was through.

This simple act of kindness impacted my life in a dramatic way. I do not remember what he looked like and will never see him again, but his kindness will always be remembered as a life changing event for me.

Random acts of kindness are what bring purpose and meaning to our lives. It's through everyday thoughts and actions and simple exchanges with others that bring not only our own lives meaning, but for others as well.

A smile can save a life. A kind gesture, a thoughtful word, everyday exchanges, are what's meaningful. Sometimes in life we get lost in the big picture to the extent that we lose meaning in everyday purpose.

Helping others through their journeys is what this earth experience is all about. Sometimes we will never know if we have helped someone or not, but that doesn't matter. Maybe the purpose of life is simply to be kind.

Everything has Purpose

Every life experience, every interaction, every incident, serves a purpose. The harder the experience, the more significant the lesson.

There is purpose in healing and recovery. Sometimes the purpose of illness, grief or loss is for the living or perhaps for those connected to a sick person. It is during these times that illness can create a lot of chaos and change. It can break families apart or it can bring them together depending on the level of dysfunction.

Relationships teach us a lot about ourselves in either positive or negative ways. Being aware, we can differentiate lessons and learn from them.

Purpose and the search for meaning are universal in that we all seek a reason for living. We don't all travel the same roads or pathways in life, but we all need to feel our lives matter.

As with difficult life lessons, we are given opportunities in life to make a difference. Sometimes we are so lost in the search for purpose and meaning that we do not see what or who is in need at the moment.

Sometimes it's not about what we are searching for but what we give. Our time, our energy, our kindness, all have purpose.

Being in the present moment makes life meaningful.

Career is only one way to find purpose. There are thousands of other pathways that can lead us to finding meaning in our lives if we are willing to travel them.

Don't get lost in the search; there is no promise of another day.

There are endless ways to lIve a meaningful life.

Remember when you are feeling lost and directionless: breathe, be present, find purpose in the moment. Moments are all we have.

THE END

Made in the USA
Las Vegas, NV
06 September 2022